Empowering your leadership mindset 2.0

The ultimate guide to reaching your full potential

By

Sterling Forbes

Copyright

Table of Content

Introduction

An initiative outlook includes having specific perspectives, convictions and assumptions that make the underpinning of what your identity is, how you lead others and how you collaborate with and impact your partners.

This attitude is critical to sharpening because it is the driving part of all that you take care of inside your business. It administers your viewpoints, choices and activities, and it influences everybody around you in the workplace. Your thinking designs impact your relationship with others, how you accomplish your objectives and the progress of your general presentation.

A few qualities make up the best initiative mindset. Understanding what some of them are and why they are significant can assist you with understanding how to create and reinforce your initiative attitude

Eagerness to Face Difficulties

One of the main components of an initiative outlook is to not be reluctant to deal with difficulties and meet them directly all things being equal. A pioneer will proactively recognize hindrances and casing them as any open doors for examples and development. At the point when a circumstance becomes troublesome, a person with an initiative methodology will uphold their partners and assist them with staying zeroed in on the ultimate objective. An authority disposition will permit you to keep progress moving while at the same time keeping up with your group's spirit in any circumstance.

Humbleness

Being a decent pioneer is a fragile harmony between certainty and lowliness. It very well may be hard to persuade representatives to follow the individuals who appear to be powerless or uninvolved inside their association. All the while, barely any individuals need to manage a pompous pioneer.

An ideal authority disposition will put you directly in the centre. It will permit you to be somebody who won't hesitate to concede when they are off-base and will put forth a valiant effort to deal with their weaknesses. It will likewise empower you to esteem and consider the contemplations, abilities and commitments of everybody in the work environment, regardless of their situation in the organization effectively.

attributes are two essential components to being trusted and regarded. Consider minutes when you might have run over somebody you believed you were unable to trust or open up to. Circumstances like these may achieve sensations of inconvenience that you would prefer not to have. A similar idea goes for the working environment, particularly when you're in an administrative role.

Your partners ought to feel like they can trust you and examine almost anything with you on the off chance that it implies taking care of an issue or making enhancements. You ought to continuously endeavour to be transparent with them. A believed pioneer cultivates positive associations with partners, prompting upgrades in mindset and efficiency at work.

Acknowledgement of Obligation

A pioneer ought to exhibit honesty and own up to their activities to construct trust among individuals around them. A decent pioneer imparts working environment victories and accomplishments to every one of their partners, guaranteeing the credit is uniformly disseminated and not exclusively given to any one individual. If anything turns out badly inside the organization, a positive chief will acknowledge full liability to pursue an answer to cure it.

They see it as a growth opportunity and make a solid effort to comprehend what enhancements can be made and how can be based upon these improvements later on. Taking responsibility is a critical part of the initiative outlook about critical thinking.

Veritable Interest in Others' Prosperity

With their associates, positive pioneers need to see them develop and prevail in the entirety of their undertakings. Pioneers ought to have the option to perceive when to carve out an opportunity to see any battles associates might be encountering, whether these happen inside or outside of the working environment. A little strong but fair affection can do wonders in specific occasions where you as a pioneer are in a situation to have a sincere talk with a partner in regards to their exhibition.

You don't need to be excessively gruff while giving your criticism, however, you ought to recognize pertinent regions that could involve a lift in execution. All things considered, it will be challenging for somebody to make upgrades assuming they know nothing about their inadequacies.

Perceiving everybody's endeavours and achievements is additionally significant. Doing so causes each person to feel seen and appreciated for all the difficult work they do. Showing veritable appreciation to your workers can convince them to keep giving their work their absolute maximum effort.

Chapter 1: The Power of Leadership Mindset

In today's dynamic and ever-evolving world, leadership is no longer confined to titles and positions—it's a mindset that fuels transformation and drives success. Welcome to the journey of Empowering Your Leadership Mindset 2.0: The Ultimate Guide to Reaching Your Full Potential.

Introducing the Concept of Leadership Mindset

Imagine two leaders facing a similar challenge. One leader, driven by a fixed mindset, sees obstacles as insurmountable barriers. They're wary of change and shy away from taking risks. The other leader, embracing a growth mindset, views challenges as opportunities for growth. They're open to learning, adaptable, and driven to overcome obstacles. This is the essence of Leadership Mindset 2.0.

Maria, a successful CEO who attributes her achievements to her growth mindset. Early in her career, she faced a major setback when a product launch failed. Rather than dwelling on failure, Maria saw it as a chance to learn. She led her team through a post-mortem analysis, identifying valuable lessons that shaped future successes.

Take a moment to reflect on your approach to challenges. Are you more inclined to see them as roadblocks or as stepping stones? Jot down an example of a recent challenge you faced and how your mindset influenced your response.

Leadership Mindset operates on a spectrum, with fixed and growth mindsets at opposite ends. Where do you currently fall on this spectrum? The good news is that mindsets are not fixed; they can be cultivated and shifted.

Thomas Edison, known for inventing the lightbulb, demonstrated a remarkable growth mindset. He famously said, "I have not failed. I've just found 10,000 ways that won't work." Edison's relentless curiosity and willingness to experiment led to one of history's most impactful innovations.

As you embark on this journey, remember that curiosity is the cornerstone of a growth mindset. Embrace challenges as opportunities to learn and experiment. The more you cultivate curiosity, the more you'll empower your leadership mindset.

Your mindset sets the tone for your leadership journey. Leadership Mindset 2.0

is about embracing challenges, fostering curiosity, and growing through adversity. As we delve deeper into this guide, you'll uncover strategies and tools to transform your approach to leadership and propel you toward your full potential.

Understanding the Impact of Mindset on Leadership Success

As you embark on the journey of Empowering Your Leadership Mindset, it's essential to recognize the profound impact that your mindset has on your effectiveness as a leader. The way you perceive yourself, your abilities, and the challenges you encounter shapes your actions and outcomes.

Consider the story of Jane, a mid-level manager. With a fixed mindset, Jane believed that her abilities were static and couldn't change. When she was assigned a high-stakes project, she hesitated, fearing failure. This fear influenced her decisions, leading to missed opportunities and suboptimal outcomes.

Recall a situation where your mindset influenced your decisions and actions. How did your beliefs about your capabilities impact the outcome? What could have been different with a different mindset?

On the flip side, leaders with a growth mindset like Alex understand that abilities can be developed through effort and learning. When Alex faced a similar high-stakes project, he embraced the challenge, saw setbacks as learning opportunities, and sought guidance from mentors and peers. This approach led to innovation and success.

Serena Williams, the legendary tennis player, embodies a growth mindset. She embraces challenges and failures as opportunities to refine her skills. Serena's dedication to learning and improvement has contributed to her enduring dominance in her sport.

To foster a growth mindset, start by reframing failures as stepping stones and challenges as opportunities. Embrace setbacks as chances to learn and improve. Emphasize effort and resilience over innate talent, both in yourself and in your team.

Your leadership mindset ripples through your team and organization. A leader's beliefs and behaviours set the tone for the culture, affecting collaboration, innovation, and employee engagement. By modelling a growth mindset, you encourage your team to take risks, learn from failures, and continuously improve.

Your mindset is a lens through which you perceive the world and approach leadership. Recognizing the power of your beliefs is the first step toward becoming an empowered leader.

Setting the Stage for Your Journey to Empowered Leadership

Welcome to a transformative journey of self-discovery and growth, where we explore the depths of Empowering Your Leadership Mindset. In this chapter, we'll lay the foundation for your path to becoming an empowered leader by understanding the key elements that shape your mindset.

A leadership mindset is not a fixed trait; it's a dynamic force that evolves. Think of it as a mental compass that guides your decisions, behaviours, and interactions. As you embark on this journey, remember that your mindset is a canvas waiting to be painted with intention and purpose.

Take a moment to assess your current leadership mindset. Are there areas where you lean more toward a fixed mindset? Are there aspects where you naturally embrace growth? Creating awareness around these tendencies is the first step toward intentional change.

Consider the story of Michael, a manager who transitioned from a fixed mindset to a growth mindset. Initially, Michael believed he had to have all the answers. When he shifted his perspective to one of growth, he became comfortable seeking input from his team, valuing diverse perspectives, and embracing continuous learning.

Pixar, the animation studio behind beloved films, fosters a culture of innovation through its growth mindset principles. Their mindset encourages calculated risks, learning from mistakes, and embracing creative challenges, resulting in groundbreaking storytelling and cinematic magic.

Begin your journey by recognizing moments when your mindset influences your decisions. Take note of situations where you could benefit from a growth mindset perspective. Challenge yourself to ask, "How can I approach this with a willingness to learn and improve?"

Your mindset drives your actions, and your actions reinforce your mindset. This reciprocal relationship forms the cornerstone of effective leadership. By consciously aligning your thoughts and behaviours with an empowered mindset, you amplify your leadership impact.

As we set the stage for your journey to empowered leadership, remember that your mindset is a powerful tool. Your beliefs about your abilities, challenges, and growth potential shape your leadership narrative. In the upcoming chapters, we'll delve deeper into specific aspects of leadership mindset, equipping you with tools and strategies to lead with intention and impact.

In Chapter 2, we'll explore the critical role of self-awareness in nurturing an empowered leadership mindset. Get ready to uncover the layers of your authentic self and harness your strengths for leadership success.

Chapter 2: Self-Awareness and Growth

Exploring Your Current Mindset and Self-Perception

Welcome to Chapter 2, where we embark on a journey of self-discovery and growth. Self-awareness is the cornerstone of effective leadership, and in this chapter, we'll uncover the power of examining your current mindset and self-perception.

Imagine your mindset as a pair of glasses through which you view the world. Sometimes, these glasses can distort how you see yourself as a leader. This distortion can lead to missed opportunities and self-limiting beliefs.

Take a few moments to visualize your leadership journey so far. What beliefs do you hold about your abilities and potential? Are there moments when self-doubt has held you back? Write down these thoughts and reflect on their impact on your decisions and actions.

David, a manager thought he had to have all the answers. He believed a leader should know everything and hesitated to ask for help. By recognizing this fixed mindset, David started seeking input from his team, fostering collaboration, and creating an environment of continuous learning.

Maria, an aspiring leader, struggled with imposter syndrome—an internal belief that she didn't deserve her success. Through self-awareness, Maria identified this mindset and worked to reframe it. With time, she embraced her achievements and led with newfound confidence.

Start a journal to document your thoughts and reflections about your leadership journey. Regular journaling helps you uncover patterns, identify areas for growth, and celebrate your progress.

Your mindset influences your self-perception, and your self-perception reinforces your mindset. This loop shapes how you lead. By understanding this connection, you gain the power to intentionally mould your leadership identity.

As you develop self-awareness, you gain the ability to lead from a place of authenticity. Embracing your strengths and acknowledging your growth areas allows you to connect more deeply with your team.

This chapter marks the beginning of a transformative journey—one where you'll peel back the layers of your leadership mindset. By exploring your current beliefs, you're taking a step toward becoming an empowered leader.

Embracing a Growth Mindset for Personal and Professional Development

In the quest for empowered leadership, a growth mindset is your most powerful tool. It's the belief that your abilities and intelligence can be developed through effort, learning, and perseverance. In this section, we'll explore how embracing a growth mindset can elevate your leadership journey.

Imagine you're a gardener cultivating a mindset garden. A growth mindset is like planting seeds of potential. With nurturing and care, these seeds bloom into a forest of continuous learning and improvement.

Visualize yourself as a gardener of your mindset. What "seeds" do you want to plant? What areas of your leadership do you want to develop? Write down these areas and commit to nurturing them over time.

Mia is a leader who once viewed challenges as roadblocks. As she embraced a growth mindset, challenges became stepping stones. Mia saw setbacks as learning experiences, inspiring innovative solutions and resilience in the face of adversity.

Wilbur and Orville Wright, pioneers of aviation, exemplified a growth mindset. They faced numerous failures and setbacks while attempting to build the first successful aeroplane. Their unwavering belief in the potential for improvement drove them to learn from each trial and ultimately achieve their goal.

When faced with a challenge, remind yourself that you simply haven't mastered it "yet." This shift in perspective opens the door to learning and growth, transforming obstacles into opportunities.

Your mindset doesn't just shape your thoughts; it shapes your actions. With a growth mindset, you're more likely to take on challenges, seek feedback, and invest in your development.

Leaders who cultivate a growth mindset encourage their teams to do the same. By showing vulnerability, admitting mistakes, and demonstrating a commitment to improvement, you set the stage for a culture of continuous learning.

Embracing a growth mindset is the foundation for becoming an empowered leader. It's the belief that your potential is limitless and that every experience—whether a success or setback—is an opportunity to learn and evolve.

Leveraging Self-Awareness to Drive Leadership Effectiveness

In this section, we'll delve into how self-awareness, when coupled with a growth mindset, becomes a dynamic force propelling leadership effectiveness and fostering deep connections.

Imagine self-awareness as a mirror reflecting not just your appearance, but your inner thoughts, emotions, and intentions. This mirror unveils how others perceive you and shed light on your impact on your team.

Recall a recent interaction with a team member. Consider their perception of you versus your intended impression. This exercise helps pinpoint areas where your intentions align with impact and where adjustments are needed.

Alex is a leader who believed in approachability. Through self-awareness, he realized his tendency to offer solutions undermined his team's growth. Shifting gears, Alex started asking probing questions that empowered his team to find solutions independently.

Laura, a project manager, once avoided conflict at all costs. Self-awareness revealed the toll on team dynamics. By addressing this, Laura learned conflict resolution skills, transforming her team into an open and communicative unit.

End each day reflecting on interactions. Did your actions match your intentions? Did you exhibit active listening and empathy? This simple routine enhances self-awareness in real-time.

Leaders who understand their impact foster trust and open communication. Acknowledging strengths and areas for growth encourages your team to embrace the journey alongside you.

Self-awareness isn't just a concept—it's a tool for effective leadership. Coupled with a growth mindset, it becomes a compass guiding decisions, actions, and interactions.

In Chapter 3, we'll explore the role of effective communication in nurturing an empowered leadership mindset. Discover how your words and interactions shape leadership impact.

Chapter 3: The Role of Communication in Influential Leadership

Effective communication is the bedrock of influential leadership. In this chapter, we delve into how your communication style, influenced by your mindset, shapes your leadership impact and fosters meaningful connections.

Think of communication as a bridge that connects your thoughts to the hearts and minds of your team. The words you choose, the tone you use, and your active listening skills are all key components of this art.

Recall a recent conversation where your message may not have landed as intended. Reflect on the words you used, your tone, and the outcome. This exercise helps uncover areas where you can fine-tune your communication approach.

Imagine you're delivering a presentation, and a sudden technical glitch derails your flow. A growth mindset urges you to adapt, think on your feet, and turn this challenge into an opportunity to connect authentically with your audience.

Anna, a team leader, embraced mindful communication. She noticed that her initial habit of interrupting team members stifled collaboration. With self-awareness and a growth mindset, Anna learned to listen actively, encouraging diverse perspectives.

In conversations, practice the "power of pause." This brief moment of reflection allows you to respond thoughtfully, enhancing the quality of your communication.

Language shapes your leadership narrative. A growth mindset prompts you to replace phrases like "I can't" with "I'm working on it." This shift in language fosters an environment of continuous improvement.

As we conclude this chapter, remember that communication isn't just about words—it's about connecting, engaging, and influencing. By aligning your communication approach with a growth mindset, you set the stage for impactful leadership.

Active Listening, Empathetic Connection, and Effective Expression

Within the realm of influential leadership, the art of communication extends beyond words—it encompasses active listening, empathetic connection, and effective expression. This chapter delves into how these components, influenced by your growth mindset, elevate your leadership impact.

Imagine a conversation as a symphony. Active listening is the conductor that harmonizes the notes, ensuring every voice is heard. By fully engaging in the conversation, you signal respect and value for your team's contributions.

In your next conversation, challenge yourself to listen more actively. Focus on understanding the speaker's message without immediately formulating a response. Notice how this shifts the dynamic of the conversation.

Empathy involves more than understanding—it's about feeling and connecting on an emotional level. As a growth-minded leader, you recognize that acknowledging and valuing others' emotions builds trust and rapport.

Jake, a manager, learned the power of empathy when a team member faced personal challenges. By lending a listening ear and offering support, Jake not only strengthened the team member's loyalty but also enhanced team cohesion.

Set aside time each day to reflect on interactions from an empathetic perspective. How might the other person have felt? What emotions were at play? This practice nurtures your empathetic connection.

A growth mindset guides your expression, encouraging clarity, and constructive delivery. Whether giving praise, addressing challenges, or presenting ideas, effective expression ensures your message resonates.

As we conclude this chapter, remember that communication is a multifaceted tool. Active listening, empathy, and effective expression weave together to create a tapestry of connection and understanding.

Creating a Culture of Clear and Open Communication

Effective leadership communication goes beyond individual interactions—it shapes the very culture of your team or organization. This chapter explores how a growth mindset, combined with clear and open communication, fosters an environment of collaboration and trust.

Imagine transparent communication as a pebble dropped into a pond, creating ripples that spread far and wide. When leaders communicate openly, they set a precedent for transparency, encouraging team members to do the same.

Think of a recent situation where transparent communication could have improved outcomes. Reflect on how you could have shared more information and the potential impact it might have had.

Leaders who communicate openly build trust by valuing their team's input and being honest about successes and challenges. This transparency establishes a foundation of trust that enhances team cohesion and engagement.

Maria is a manager, who faced tough decisions during a company reorganization. By openly sharing the reasons behind the changes and acknowledging the uncertainty, she not only gained her team's understanding but also their commitment to weathering the transition together.

Regularly hold open forums where team members can share their thoughts, concerns, and ideas. This two-way communication fosters a sense of ownership and engagement among team members.

A growth mindset leads to conversations that focus on development. Leaders with this mindset encourage team members to share their goals, challenges, and aspirations, fostering an environment of continuous learning.

As this chapter concludes, remember that communication isn't just a tool—it's the very essence of your team's culture. By embracing clear, open, and transparent communication, you set the stage for a collaborative and trusting environment.

In Chapter 4, we'll delve into the art of effective decision-making. Explore how your mindset influences your choices and how cultivating a growth mindset can lead to informed and confident decisions.

Chapter 4: Decision-Making for Impact

In the intricate tapestry of leadership, decision-making stands as a pivotal thread. This chapter delves into the art of making confident and strategic decisions, exploring how your mindset shapes the choices you make and the impact they have on your leadership journey.

Picture decision-making as a landscape where every choice shapes the terrain of your leadership path. Your mindset is the compass guiding you through this landscape, influencing whether you tread familiar paths or venture into uncharted territories.

Consider your past decisions as a leader. Were there instances where a fixed mindset held you back from taking bold steps? Reflect on how a growth mindset might have altered the outcomes.

Confident decision-making is born from a foundation of self-assuredness and competence. A growth mindset bolsters this confidence by encouraging you to embrace challenges and learn from setbacks. Paired with strategic thinking, confident decisions lead to impactful outcomes.

Maria, a CEO, faced a crucial crossroads that demanded a bold choice. Her growth mindset empowered her to view the decision as an opportunity for innovation rather than a potential pitfall. She blended this with a strategic approach, analyzing data and seeking input before making her move.

Start a decision journal to document the major choices you make. Reflect on your thought process, the factors you considered, and the mindset that guided your decision. Over time, this journal becomes a valuable resource for refining your decision-making skills.

Strategic decisions involve a blend of analytical thinking and intuition. A growth mindset encourages you to trust your instincts while also seeking data-driven insights. This synergy helps you navigate complexity with clarity.

As this chapter concludes, remember that decisions are the building blocks of your leadership legacy. By embracing a growth mindset and strategic thinking, you shape the trajectory of your journey and the impact you leave behind.

Balancing Analytical Thinking with Intuition

As you traverse the landscape of decision-making, the interplay between analytical thinking and intuition takes centre stage. Your growth mindset acts as the conductor, harmonizing these distinct approaches into impactful choices.

Imagine analytical thinking as the architect of decisions, meticulously crafting blueprints based on data. Intuition, the artist, paints in shades of insight and experience. Your growth mindset embraces both, recognizing their inherent value.

Recall a recent decision. Reflect on the roles analytical thinking and intuition played. Consider how a different balance might have influenced the outcome.

Intuition isn't a mere hunch—it draws from your experiences and observations. A growth mindset encourages you to trust this wellspring of insights, especially in complex situations.

Alex is a manager facing market shifts. While data pointed one way, his intuition suggested an alternative. Trusting his growth mindset, he combined data with intuition for a successful adaptation strategy.

Before significant decisions, tune into your intuition. Ask: What does my gut feeling suggest? How does it align with the data? This practice nurtures a balanced perspective.

Balanced leaders make decisions grounded in evidence and enriched by insight. This approach empowers you to navigate complexity with clarity.

Decisions are a symphony—a harmonious blend of analysis and intuition conducted by your growth mindset. This fusion yields choices that resonate with impact.

Navigating Uncertainty and Complex Choices

In the dynamic world of leadership, uncertainty and complexity are constants. This chapter explores how your growth mindset equips you to navigate the intricate web of uncertain situations and make sense of complex choices.

Imagine uncertainty as a fog that obscures your path. Your growth mindset acts as a compass, guiding you through the haze by embracing ambiguity and seeking learning opportunities.

Reflect on times when uncertainty led to discomfort. How did your mindset shape your response? Consider how a growth mindset might have enabled you to embrace the unknown with curiosity and resilience.

Complex choices resemble a puzzle with numerous pieces. Your growth mindset views these puzzles as opportunities for growth rather than sources of stress. This perspective empowers you to break down complexity into manageable steps.

Maria is a leader facing a major restructuring. Her growth mindset encouraged her to view this complexity as a chance to learn. She engaged her team, fostering collaboration that led to innovative solutions.

Amid the uncertainty, make learning a priority. Seek out new perspectives, acquire new skills, and adapt your approach based on emerging information. Your growth mindset propels you to thrive in change.

Consider the metaphor of a chess game. Just as a skilled player anticipates various moves, your growth mindset enables you to anticipate potential outcomes and adapt your strategy accordingly.

As you conclude this chapter, remember that uncertainty and complexity are not obstacles but growth opportunities. Your growth mindset equips you to navigate uncharted territories and make informed choices.

Chapter 5: Resilience and Adaptability

Building Resilience to Thrive in Challenging Environments

In the crucible of leadership, challenges and setbacks are inevitable. This chapter illuminates the profound role of your growth mindset in cultivating resilience and embracing adaptability to not just weather storms, but to thrive amidst them.

Imagine resilience as the foundation of a study tree, firmly rooted in your growth mindset. As storms of adversity rage, your mindset provides stability, allowing you to bend without breaking.

Recall a significant setback you've faced as a leader. How did your mindset influence your response? Reflect on how a growth mindset might have enabled you to view the setback as a stepping stone rather than an obstacle.

Adaptability is the chameleon-like ability to adjust and thrive in changing circumstances. A growth mindset fosters this trait by encouraging you to see change as an opportunity for growth rather than a threat.

Alex is a leader navigating a rapidly evolving industry. With a growth mindset, he embraced continuous learning, empowering him to lead his team through transitions with confidence.

In challenging environments, your growth mindset propels you to ask, "What can I learn from this experience?" By seeking lessons even in adversity, you transform setbacks into opportunities for growth.

Consider the metaphor of a river. Your growth mindset allows you to flow around obstacles rather than resist them. This adaptability ensures a constant forward momentum, even in the face of challenges.

As you conclude this chapter, remember that resilience and adaptability are the cornerstones of effective leadership. Your growth mindset equips you to not only endure challenges but to emerge stronger and more agile.

Embracing Change and Leading Through Ambiguity

In the crucible of leadership, challenges and setbacks are inevitable. This chapter illuminates the profound role of your growth mindset in cultivating resilience and embracing adaptability to not just weather storms, but to thrive amidst them.

Imagine resilience as the foundation of a sturdy tree, firmly rooted in your growth mindset. As storms of adversity rage, your mindset provides stability, allowing you to bend without breaking.

Recall a significant setback you've faced as a leader. How did your mindset influence your response? Reflect on how a growth mindset might have enabled you to view the setback as a stepping stone rather than an obstacle.

Adaptability is the chameleon-like ability to adjust and thrive in changing circumstances. A growth mindset fosters this trait by encouraging you to see change as an opportunity for growth rather than a threat.

Alex is a leader navigating a rapidly evolving industry. With a growth mindset, he embraced continuous learning, empowering him to lead his team through transitions with confidence.

In challenging environments, your growth mindset propels you to ask, "What can I learn from this experience?" By seeking lessons even in adversity, you transform setbacks into opportunities for growth.

Consider the metaphor of a river. Your growth mindset allows you to flow around obstacles rather than resist them. This adaptability ensures a constant forward momentum, even in the face of challenges.

As you conclude this chapter, remember that resilience and adaptability are the cornerstones of effective leadership. Your growth mindset equips you to not only endure challenges but to emerge stronger and more agile.

Transforming Setbacks into Stepping Stones

In the crucible of leadership, challenges and setbacks are inevitable. This chapter illuminates the profound role of your growth mindset in cultivating resilience and embracing adaptability to not just weather storms, but to thrive amidst them.

Imagine resilience as the foundation of a sturdy tree, firmly rooted in your growth mindset. As storms of adversity rage, your mindset provides stability, allowing you to bend without breaking.

Recall a significant setback you've faced as a leader. How did your mindset influence your response? Reflect on how a growth mindset might have enabled you to view the setback as a stepping stone rather than an obstacle.

Adaptability is the chameleon-like ability to adjust and thrive in changing circumstances. A growth mindset fosters this trait by encouraging you to see change as an opportunity for growth rather than a threat.

Alex is a leader navigating a rapidly evolving industry. With a growth mindset, he embraced continuous learning, empowering him to lead his team through transitions with confidence.

In challenging environments, your growth mindset propels you to ask, "What can I learn from this experience?" By seeking lessons even in adversity, you transform setbacks into opportunities for growth.

Consider the metaphor of a river. Your growth mindset allows you to flow around obstacles rather than resist them. This adaptability ensures a constant forward momentum, even in the face of challenges.

As you conclude this chapter, remember that resilience and adaptability are the cornerstones of effective leadership. Your growth mindset equips you to not only endure challenges but to emerge stronger and more agile.

In Chapter 6, we'll explore the realm of effective teamwork and collaboration. Discover how your mindset influences group dynamics and how cultivating a growth-oriented team culture can lead to unparalleled success.

Chapter 6: Empowering Teams and Collaboration

Motivating and Inspiring Your Team Toward Shared Goals

In the tapestry of effective leadership, the ability to empower teams and foster collaboration is a defining thread. This chapter delves into how your growth mindset catalyzes motivating and inspiring your team toward shared goals.

Consider your growth mindset as a beacon that illuminates the path toward collaborative success. By valuing diverse perspectives and fostering a culture of openness, you guide your team toward unified achievements.

Reflect on past instances where your leadership motivated a team toward a shared goal. How did your growth mindset contribute to this success? Consider how a growth mindset might further amplify your team's motivation.

Empowerment stems from a growth mindset that recognizes the potential within each team member. By fostering an environment where individuals are encouraged to stretch their capabilities, you cultivate a sense of ownership and initiative.

Maria is a leader who championed her team's growth. With a growth mindset, she encouraged them to embrace challenges. As her team achieved milestones, their collective motivation soared.

Inspiration, like a ripple in a pond, starts from your growth mindset and spreads throughout the team. By demonstrating passion, perseverance, and an unwavering belief in the goal, you ignite a shared sense of purpose.

Challenge your team with stretch goals—ambitious targets that encourage them to rise above the ordinary. Your growth mindset propels you to view challenges as opportunities, inspiring your team to transcend their limits.

As this chapter concludes, remember that effective leadership is not just about individual achievements, but the collective success of your team. Your growth mindset empowers you to motivate and inspire your team, leading them toward shared goals.

Nurturing a Collaborative Environment for Innovation

In the tapestry of effective leadership, the ability to empower teams and foster collaboration is a defining thread. This chapter delves into how your growth mindset catalyzes motivating and inspiring your team toward shared goals.

Consider your growth mindset as a beacon that illuminates the path toward collaborative success. By valuing diverse perspectives and fostering a culture of openness, you guide your team toward unified achievements.

Reflect on past instances where your leadership motivated a team toward a shared goal. How did your growth mindset contribute to this success? Consider how a growth mindset might further amplify your team's motivation.

Empowerment stems from a growth mindset that recognizes the potential within each team member. By fostering an environment where individuals are encouraged to stretch their capabilities, you cultivate a sense of ownership and initiative.

Maria is a leader who championed her team's growth. With a growth mindset, she encouraged them to embrace challenges. As her team achieved milestones, their collective motivation soared.

Inspiration, like a ripple in a pond, starts from your growth mindset and spreads throughout the team. By demonstrating passion, perseverance, and an unwavering belief in the goal, you ignite a shared sense of purpose.

Challenge your team with stretch goals—ambitious targets that encourage them to rise above the ordinary. Your growth mindset propels you to view challenges as opportunities, inspiring your team to transcend their limits.

As this chapter concludes, remember that effective leadership is not just about individual achievements, but the collective success of your team. Your growth mindset empowers you to motivate and inspire your team, leading them toward shared goals.

Recognizing and Harnessing the Strengths of Individuals

In the intricate mosaic of leadership, empowering teams and nurturing collaboration is a vibrant thread. This chapter delves into how your growth mindset becomes a dynamic force, enabling you to recognize and harness the unique strengths of individuals within your team.

Imagine your growth mindset as a prism that refracts the diverse talents of your team members into a spectrum of possibilities. By acknowledging and celebrating individual strengths, you create a harmonious symphony of collective excellence.

Recall instances where your leadership enabled team members to shine through their strengths. How did your growth mindset play a pivotal role in fostering such an environment? Consider how further embracing this mindset could enhance your team's cohesion.

Empowerment flourishes when you view each team member as a tapestry of strengths waiting to be woven together. Your growth mindset inspires you to create an environment where these strengths are recognized, nurtured, and woven into the fabric of success.

Maria is a leader who excelled at harnessing individual strengths. By identifying and leveraging the unique talents of her team members, she created a dynamic and collaborative workspace that yielded remarkable results.

As a leader, your growth mindset fuels you to be a strengths-based champion. By highlighting and encouraging the application of individual strengths, you foster a sense of fulfillment and accomplishment among team members.

Challenge yourself to unlock the full potential of your team by intentionally aligning tasks with their strengths. Your growth mindset guides you to orchestrate roles that empower team members to shine in areas where they naturally excel.

As this chapter draws to a close, remember that effective leadership is not just about guiding a team, but about amplifying the brilliance of each individual within it. Your growth mindset serves as the compass guiding you to recognize and harness these strengths.

In Chapter 7, we embark on the final leg of your journey—one of reflection and continuation. Discover how to sustain growth, nurture your leadership mindset, and leave an indelible mark on the landscape of leadership.

Chapter 7: Continuous Growth and Legacy

Cultivating a Lifelong Learning Mindset for Ongoing Improvement

In this final chapter, we embark on a journey that transcends leadership and stretches into the realms of continuous growth and legacy. Your growth mindset, the cornerstone of your leadership journey, evolves into a catalyst for lasting impact.

Imagine your growth mindset as a wellspring of endless possibilities, a source of perpetual renewal. As a leader, you're not bound by the status quo but fueled by an insatiable curiosity and thirst for knowledge.

Reflect on your leadership journey so far. How has your growth mindset fueled your pursuit of continuous improvement? Consider how embracing a lifelong learning mindset could amplify your impact and shape your legacy.

Legacy isn't a monument; it's the indelible mark you leave through the lives you touch and the transformations you inspire. Your growth mindset fosters an enduring legacy by constantly seeking ways to uplift and elevate those around you.

Meet Daniel, a leader who exemplified the fusion of a growth mindset and legacy. His commitment to continuous learning rippled through his team, inspiring them to become lifelong learners themselves.

Nurture your legacy by becoming a beacon of learning. Encourage your team to embrace growth, and create an environment where learning isn't an option but an inherent part of the culture.

Challenge yourself to set personal goals for continuous learning. Whether it's mastering a new skill, exploring a different domain, or deepening your existing expertise, your growth mindset thrives in the pursuit of knowledge.

As this chapter concludes, remember that your legacy is not static; it's a dynamic force that evolves with each step you take. Your growth mindset fuels your journey of continuous growth and inspires others to follow suit.

With this, we conclude our exploration into leadership empowerment, growth, and legacy. May your path be illuminated by the light of learning, and may your legacy be a testament to the transformation that a dedicated growth mindset can bring.

Crafted with narratives of aspiration, exercises of introspection, and insights of impact, this chapter serves as your guide to cultivating a lifelong learning mindset. Use it to shape your legacy and pave the way for a brighter, empowered future.

Setting Personal and Professional Goals for Sustainable Success

In this final chapter, we embark on a journey that transcends leadership and stretches into the realms of continuous growth and legacy. Your growth mindset, the cornerstone of your leadership journey, evolves into a catalyst for lasting impact.

Imagine your growth mindset as a wellspring of endless possibilities, a source of perpetual renewal. As a leader, you're not bound by the status quo but fueled by an insatiable curiosity and thirst for knowledge.

Reflect on your leadership journey so far. How has your growth mindset fueled your pursuit of continuous improvement? Consider how embracing a lifelong learning mindset could amplify your impact and shape your legacy.

Legacy isn't a monument; it's the indelible mark you leave through the lives you touch and the transformations you inspire. Your growth mindset fosters an enduring legacy by constantly seeking ways to uplift and elevate those around you.

Consider the story of Daniel, a leader who exemplified the fusion of a growth mindset and legacy. His commitment to continuous learning rippled through his team, inspiring them to become lifelong learners themselves.

Nurture your legacy by becoming a beacon of learning. Encourage your team to embrace growth, and create an environment where learning isn't an option but an inherent part of the culture.

Challenge yourself to set personal goals for continuous learning. Whether it's mastering a new skill, exploring a different domain, or deepening your existing expertise, your growth mindset thrives in the pursuit of knowledge.

As this chapter concludes, remember that your legacy is not static; it's a dynamic force that evolves with each step you take. Your growth mindset fuels your journey of continuous growth and inspires others to follow suit.

With this, we conclude our exploration into leadership empowerment, growth, and legacy. May your path be illuminated by the light of learning, and may your legacy be a testament to the transformation that a dedicated growth mindset can bring.

Crafted with narratives of aspiration, exercises of introspection, and insights of impact, this chapter serves as your guide to setting personal and professional goals for sustainable success. Use it to shape your legacy and pave the way for a brighter, empowered future.

Leaving a Positive and Lasting Leadership Legacy

In this final chapter, we embark on a journey that transcends leadership and stretches into the realms of continuous growth and legacy. Your growth mindset, the cornerstone of your leadership journey, evolves into a catalyst for lasting impact.

Imagine your growth mindset as a wellspring of endless possibilities, a source of perpetual renewal. As a leader, you're not bound by the status quo but fueled by an insatiable curiosity and thirst for knowledge.

Reflect on your leadership journey so far. How has your growth mindset fueled your pursuit of continuous improvement? Consider how embracing a lifelong learning mindset could amplify your impact and shape your legacy.

Legacy isn't a monument; it's the indelible mark you leave through the lives you touch and the transformations you inspire. Your growth mindset fosters an enduring legacy by constantly seeking ways to uplift and elevate those around you.

Consider the story of Daniel, a leader who exemplified the fusion of a growth mindset and legacy. His commitment to continuous learning rippled through his team, inspiring them to become lifelong learners themselves.

Nurture your legacy by becoming a beacon of learning. Encourage your team to embrace growth, and create an environment where learning isn't an option but an inherent part of the culture.

Challenge yourself to set personal goals for continuous learning. Whether it's mastering a new skill, exploring a different domain, or deepening your existing expertise, your growth mindset thrives in the pursuit of knowledge.

As this chapter concludes, remember that your legacy is not static; it's a dynamic force that evolves with each step you take. Your growth mindset fuels your journey of continuous growth and inspires others to follow suit.

With this, we conclude our exploration into leadership empowerment, growth, and legacy. Your journey doesn't end here; it's the foundation for the legacy you're building. May your path be illuminated by the light of learning, and may your legacy be a testament to the transformation that a dedicated growth mindset can bring.

Crafted with narratives of aspiration, exercises of introspection, and insights of impact, this chapter serves as your guide to leaving a positive and lasting leadership legacy. Use it to shape your legacy and pave the way for a brighter, empowered future that resonates through the annals of time.

www.ingramcontent.com/pod-product-compliance
Lightning Source LLC
Chambersburg PA
CBHW062245290526
45794CB00006B/2414